# Texas Longhorns

## A Short Essay

By

**Jim Hodges**

**Photo**: *Ms. John Wayne*, center, Alamo Village Bracketville, Texas 1967. She was a favorite of John Wayne during the filming of the movie, *The Alamo*, and was appropriately named. Photo by Jim Hodges.

# Preface

Good morning my good friends, and wishing you the best of coffee as you start this day! I had to share some beautiful thoughts, memories, art, history, and photos of our beloved Texas Longhorn cattle. Named by Man, and created by God, which is fitting in my view. They are truly historic, nostalgic, and created by the natural process. As a young cowboy, I was always caught staring at their beauty and majesty...they belong here on the wide plains and lush grasslands...they are a part of the landscape. Sipping my morning coffee and enjoying the color contrasts and sharp detailed definition, and remembering sitting astride a finely bred American Quarter Horse and gazing at each one of them as a different canvas...a star of their own show in the grandest of productions. I hope you all enjoy this simple and short essay of our beloved Texas Longhorns, and leave with some inspiration and maybe learn something as well!

# Foreword

Many years ago, when I was a mere slip of what I was to become, I experienced childhood in my home state of Kentucky. However, I grew up feeling like my heart belonged to Texas and the old west. Everything about the west; cowboys, the creak and smell of leather, cattle drives, shoot 'em ups, longhorn cattle, and of course horses intrigued me. I embraced and chased those visions, quite intent upon this pursuit of the cowboy life. Life, war, and growth got in the way but I never truly gave up on my dreams.

In my make-believe world, I lived the life of the cowboy daily. Most of the pictures taken of me in my young life show me wearing a cowboy hat, six-shooters on each hip, a vest, and chaps, always tipping that hat to the ladies and saying yes ma'am and no sir. I experienced this life vicariously but in my young mind, it seemed as real as life itself. Later I became a horseman and a stableman, but I never ascended to the high level of being a true cowboy. I did however manage to live by the discipline, honor, and example of these true Americans.

There has always been something magical about viewing longhorn cattle, peacefully grazing in the light of a setting sun. When I view pictures of them, or watch movies that they play a part in, I feel an absolute peace, but even while pretending in peace, I knew the power they possessed and what they could do if they wanted to. I guess that just added to the intrigue. After all, cowboying can be a challenging life.

Fast forward a lifetime and my friend, Jim Hodges, contacted me and asked if I would be interested in reading his historical essay about longhorn cattle and writing a foreword for it. I am familiar with Jim's work because of our friendship and our parallel path's through life and I knew this was going to be a good read. I was honored that he would trust me with his words and work, but then again, old warriors learn to trust one another.  From the very first word, I was transported back to my youth, when longhorns and cattle drives were part of the future I had planned for this life.

Sit back, sip your favorite beverage, and read this informative and entertaining story about the life of longhorn cattle in America. Jim takes you back in time to a place where they were introduced to the Americas. You just might be surprised by their origins. Are they actually a breed or are they mystical beings like Skinwalkers, or are they actually spiritual storytellers of old? Although you will receive guidance, the interpretation is yours alone. Keep reading and discover what an ox is, what tipping means, and even a good description of what a cowpoke does. It is all right here, between the pages for your reading and learning enjoyment.

When you finish this read, you will know many things. Where they come from, art from their image, their place in the building of this country, their demeanor, what scars on the horns mean and so very much more. Let Jim entertain you for a bit and educate you for a lifetime.

Now, read on, this is one journey you won't want to miss. And Jim, thank you for teaching me things I never knew.

**Richard D. Rowland**, Author.


**Richard** is a two-tour veteran of the Vietnam War, a 28 year veteran of the KY State Police, and a 20+ year owner/operator of an equine facility in Kentucky. He is retired from all endeavors except for writing. When not writing, Richard mentors people diagnosed with cancer and other health challenging hurdles. www.richarddrowlandbooks.com.

# Introduction

Welcome to the realm of the Texas Longhorn. I have prepared this short essay to introduce you to their lives and characteristics, and how they blended into and graced the cowboy and ranching world before the American Civil War, and thereafter. From their first appearance on the land we now call Texas around 1691, to their current place as the world's best known and easily recognizable cattle breed, the Texas Longhorn is strikingly unique and intriguing.

I am proud to be your author and guide through this informatory essay which I constructed first in 1999 and then revised in the year, 2020. I base it on sources and other authors that I've cited within the pages, as well as my own experience riding in the cowboy world for over 50 years at this writing. I was always thirsty to read stories about Texas Longhorn cattle and to study a mix of every breed as I always wanted to own a ranch and raise cattle and good horses the old way – the real cowboy way. I was riding horses and learning about cattle at the ripe age of five years old with my grandfather, James William Herbert Hodges, or J.W. as they called him, who was one of the last of the true open range cowboys at the turn of the 20th Century. In the mid-to-late 1950s, agriculture was the center of the world, not electronics. Cowboys rode all day in the saddle and worked an honestly long day, but as the old cowboys used to say, " I'd always cry for daylight to come, so that we could mount up and work cattle again." We all love it that much.

The stories told around the cowboy campfires were life's blood to me. Just the beginning of the drop of a story from an old-timer and I was transfixed in awe, never flinching, just absorbing and learning all that I could. I knew then that our lifestyle was flickering in the sunset, and soon the grandeur of the big ranches would slowly come to an end. But I will hold onto a worthy lifestyle and tradition, and gladly be the steward that tells the living history as long as I can sit a horse and keep my thoughts in order.

Every time that I have the privilege to gaze upon a Texas Longhorn it revives the distinguished sound of the creak of the saddle, the smell of leather and horse sweat, and the visual dream of working one more honest day as a real cowboy. Aside a virtual river of cattle stretched across the rugged wide plains of Texas is my spirit and soul - collected in the dust rising up toward God to give heartfelt and honest thanks for such a privilege and lifestyle. To be - a cowboy.

I honestly hope you enjoy this short essay about my friends that wear the big wide horns and stand tall as the tales that live about them.

# Table of Contents

# Spirit of the Longhorn

The Texas Longhorn is no beast of simple hide and horn, nor are they just the generic brother of fat stock from foreign lands as volumes of scholarly work has proclaimed. No, they are spirit walkers and storytellers of olden times that appeared out of the soil, water, and wind by a blend of God's hand with the unwritten code of the western landscape. They are mystic and arguable as the term itself and cause memorable pyrexia among their enchanted admirers. The literals will scoff at my allusion, thinking I've spent too many years in the hot Texas sun, or been thrown too hard from the high dive of a strawberry roan, but please hear me out.

Texas Longhorns are spirit walkers among the native and alien peoples of the western hemisphere who depended on them for their yield of leather, bone, milk, and meat, as well as their strength to pull and carry. Many legends were born over the historical stories handed down through generations through native people and their chiefs. They honored the Longhorn for their majesty, raw and unique beauty, big horns, and their survivability through the years and tough environments. The evidence of this exists at many historical sites where the cave or rock drawings have been preserved. There, among the spiritual drawings and etchings of stars and strange people-like images of spirit walkers, you will find the Longhorn. The American Indians viewed them as a sign of good luck. They have ensnared the spiritual eye and mind of worldwide artists who have painted, carved, and sculpted them for the appreciative beholder since they first appeared on the wild, undeveloped plains.

In the post Civil War era when the Texas Longhorn was driven North on cattle drives in mass numbers and were near extinction after the turn of the Century, the Spirit of Texas, through generous and faithful leaders stepped forward to save and preserve the breed for posterity.

"Western writer J. Frank Dobie recognized the Texas Longhorn decline in the early 1920s. He felt it was important to preserve the breed that held such a significant place in Texas history. With help from businessman Sid Richardson and rancher Graves Peeler, Dobie procured a herd of typical longhorns. They donated the animals to the Texas Parks Board in 1941 as the state herd. The board placed the herd at Lake Corpus Christi State Park near Mathis. The search continued for more of the scarce longhorns. In 1942, the board placed a second herd at Lake Brownwood State Park.

As these sites were not ideal, the Texas State Parks Board began looking for a permanent home for the herd. The board chose Fort Griffin State Park (now the Texas Historical Commission's Fort Griffin State Historic Site) as the longhorns' permanent home in 1948.

The Texas Legislature recognized the herd with Senate Concurrent Resolution No. 79 on May 17, 1969."

- **Reference:** Texas Parks and Wildlife, www.tpwd.texas.gov/ official state-longhorn

Another major contributor helping save the Texas Longhorn was the famous YO Ranch in Mountain Home, Texas which was the home of many different cattle breeds over the years since its founding in 1880 by Charles Armand Schreiner who amassed 566,000 acres. The fad for fat stock in the early 20th Century caused a sharp decline in Longhorn's popularity, and at one point there were fewer of them than the Bison. Then, in 1964, descendant, Charles Armand Schreiner III, or Charlie III as he was referred to,  joined others in an attempt to save the Longhorn from extinction. Charlie III bought several head of Longhorn cattle and raised them to a herd size of approximately one thousand. He helped form the Texas Longhorn Breeder's Association of America and served as their first president as well.

**Photo:** Charles Schreiner III, and a Texas longhorn at the YO Ranch.

# Longhorns in Art

The well-known artist, Frank Reaugh, 1860 – 1945, an adopted Texan from Illinois, and a personal witness to the Longhorn on the wild frontier was referred to, quite correctly, as the *Rembrandt of the Longhorn.* In the view of many, he captured both the history and the spirit of the Longhorn in his wide, colorful, and hardscrabble landscapes. Reaugh's canvas creations perched the Longhorn precisely where it belonged in the saga of the West.

Perhaps from the colorful portrayals of Reaugh and others, poets, or bards, were inspired to write plentitudes of published works, while other prometheans created lyrics and songs that became classic tunes from the frontier days onward. Many organizations have used them as their mascots, as well as logos for businesses. Stamps, bumper stickers, t-shirts, avatars, and ball caps all appear around the world with the distinctive Texas Longhorn image. The spiritual have even created photos, or used pieces of their bone, or hide to use in various types of a phylactery.

**Painting:** *"Longhorn Overlooking The Canyon"* by Frank Reaugh.

Another artist,  El Paso, Texas native, Tom Lea, 1907 – 2001, is considered by a wide audience of critics and admirers, to be one of the Texas Masters. Lea was also spiritually connected with the West, Longhorn cattle, and cowboys, which his canvas paintings and finely detailed illustrations portray by adding action to the subjects and stories as well. He painted dynamic murals that offered the viewer both a passive and hostile version of the longhorn cattle.

**Painting:** " Stampede" by Tom Lea.  Mural at the U.S. Post Office, Odessa, Texas. Commissioned through the Section of Fine Arts,1934-1943. Fine Arts Collection, U.S. General Services Administration.

My essay would not be complete without highlighting one final Texas Master, Robert Jenkins Onderdonk, 1852 – 1917, and his portrayal of everyday life in the early stages of the West. Some of his contributions included Longhorns, of course.  In one of my favorites, he captured the market at the rear of San Fernando Church in San Antonio in the early pioneer days. On the faces of the people, your imagination can visually intrude on their humor and issues. In the background, are the trusty Texas Longhorn steers used as oxen to pull wagons and carts. All are lounging on a lazy warm, and beautiful San Antonio day. The Longhorns are as much a part of the landscape as the soil they are resting on.

**Painting**: " Market Plaza" by Robert Jenkins Onderdonk.

So, what is an ox? When a bull is castrated, they are referred to as a steer, but when they are given a job and used for their labor such as pulling wagons, carts, or plowing equipment, they are then referred to as an ox. So essentially an ox is a steer who performs work. The Longhorn was the obvious and preferred choice.

The western movies, since the rolling of the first films, have left out the usefulness of the domesticated and well trained Longhorn cattle as oxen. Other breeds were used as oxen, but none with the size, stamina, and strength of the Longhorn. Examining the photos of the early frontier you see the ox in plentiful use, as in Onderdonk's painting. By the time western movies were being made on a grand scale, the trusty family friend and laborer, the ox, had almost disappeared, replaced with the market steer for slaughter and food. So, the movie company switched to horses or mules which were still able to be found in sufficient numbers to use in their films and provided high action for thrills and spills that patrons enjoyed.

The Texas Longhorn has influenced many master artists and a bevy of those who are unknown but can't resist the temptation of trying to capture them on canvas and photos. One of those so afflicted is your author. Having begun riding horses with my grandfather and mentor at the age of 5 years old, and securing my first real job training horses and working cattle on some of the large ranches around Texas from the late 1950s, I witnessed agriculture when it was still king. Before the electronic age, and in the heyday of the big ranches when the old cowboy traditions and stories were still fresh and in most cases strictly enforced. Spending a lifetime in concert with many breeds of cattle pointed my interest to the uniqueness of the Texas Longhorn.

**Painting**: " *The Times They Are A'Changin* " Pastel on canvas by Jim Hodges. Subject, Longhorn at Alamo Village Bracketville, Texas, 1967.

**Photo**: Author, Jim Hodges has taught people from around the world about the Texas Longhorn. In the photo, Cowboy Jim is showing a foreign exchange group a small herd of Texas Longhorn yearlings while riding his cutting horse, Buck.

Their colors remind our spirit of the natural elements all posited by God onto one single motile hide, complimented by the unmatched unique majesty of their long curving horns. They live in quiet unity with Man, the Mother Earth, and many strange creatures, and have endured all of nature's pretty dangers from the flood, to famine, the terror of illness, and still – they are here. Mankind has given thanks to God for them.

**Photo:** "Longhorn Grazing" by Jim Hodges, 2016.

# Longhorns as Storytellers

The literal history brings spiritual tales of the worship of their ancestors by countless societies and takes the seekers of knowledge deep into the European continent's cattle history. Then, on to many high adventures across the waves of the mighty Atlantic Ocean with decades of Spanish explorers bringing cattle with them of heterogeneity, for food and milk. As early as the late 1400s with the landing and introduction of cattle to the western hemisphere by Christopher Columbus, and on to the early 1500s these voyages continued to land in island and inland areas leaving cattle on their peregrinations. According to the convocation of scholars, Spanish explorers began to introduce their many breeds of cattle into western cultures, and In 1521, Spanish sailor and ship's Captain, Gregorio de Villalobos defied the law that prohibited cattle trading in Mexico. Captain Villalobos sailed from Santo Domingo and with only 6 cows and a bull, landed, and distributed them in Veracruz, Mexico. Also introducing Criollo, or Spanish cattle was the Spanish explorer Hernando Cortes. He branded his herds with three crosses which was the first brand recorded in North America.

This was not the origin of branding cattle, however, far from it! Recent archeological finds of ancient Egypt prove that they were the first ranchers of cattle in recorded history, and regularly branded their cattle for identification. This custom and practice was also handed down through time and finally introduced to the Americas.

Though the majority of these stories are documented very well, some scholars and authors have offered varied interpretations of the history thereafter, citing records and documents, opinions, poetic license, and tall tales to explain the mysterious creation and first appearance of the Texas Longhorn onto the landscape. It has always been difficult for me to believe that the creation and birth of the Longhorn were accidental, as I personally witnessed the struggle of the famous King Ranch of Texas over decades to produce the Santa Gertrudis cattle breed. Without a credible counter-theory, however, I must digress and accept that thesis for now. So, I bring my literal and mystic thesis of Texas Longhorns being created and appearing on the landscape spawned from the spirits of the people and animals that combined from somewhat dubious origins as spirit walkers. Each time one gazes upon them, they cannot help but feel the bold, and adventurous spirits of the past – their daring ancestors, both man and animal.

**Historical References:**

- Will C. Barnes, "Wichita Forest Will Be Lair of Longhorns", The Cattleman, April 1926.
- James Westfall Thompson, History of Livestock Raising in the United States, 1607-1860 (Washington: U.S. Department of Agriculture, 1942).


The Texas Longhorn is also a storyteller of their origins and ancestry through their finished form. Their classroom is the wide plains and lush grasslands as well as the escarpment and arroyo. They've effectuated themselves into legend as they spread their bodies along the many trails from California to Texas, and Florida, leaving dramatic and mystic history as they blazed these rugged towpaths and left their indelible imprint upon the glory of the Old West.

"This lasting fight to subjugate the cranky, armored longhorn critters made heroes out of cowboys. The cowpuncher, for half a century or more, has enjoyed one of the most romantic reputations in the world. A tamer breed of cattle would never have given rise to the stockhand's glory. A more domestic spirit than the usual cowpoke possessed could never have battled successfully with the longhorn, though.

Just the telling of the cowboy's story, in song and story and art and movie, every year now, more than exceeds the sale value of the trail herds delivered from Texas to Montana in the best year the longhorn ever enjoyed. An estimated ten million longhorns were drained off the Texas ranges and driven up the north trails from 1866 to 1890. In the northern plains, they fattened on the fresh, deep grass left by the vanishing buffalo and other big game." (*The Longhorn of the Wichitas, 1947.*)

**Photo**: *Scars on the Horns*, Courtesy of John Bintliff.

# Scars On The Horns

Cowboys with higher intellect and deep experience took a hard look at the scars and dings on those big horns and developed a wise policy of staying clear of them. Even a pet Longhorn can casually swat at a fly and those horns can develop the force of a baseball bat in full swing! Although capable of domestication the Texas Longhorn could become truculent and carry his wild spirit to the extreme, and not even inanimate objects had best be in the way of their wrath. They could teach through acts of violence as well as their better demeanor.

The wily predators of the wild plains would usually steer clear of a Texas Longhorn mother as she would use her size, strength, and horns to defend her young, as well as herself. These momma cows are notorious and ferocious when fending off enemies of any size or description, so they need their horns on the open pasture. When cattle are shipped, however, they no longer need them, and some ranchers opted for tipping them, which was fairly common, or cutting them off, which was very rare. Most ranchers left them alone as it was time-consuming and took a lot of effort which cost them money.

Though their horns are huge and have twists and turns in them, the Texas Longhorn can navigate some of the tightest spots imaginable. In the early days of the railroad, they could be loaded into the boxcars for shipment fairly easily by cowpokes. Cowpokes, or cowpunchers were the people who worked in the shipping, and loading areas at stock pens and literally poked, or punched the cattle into the chutes, and onto the boxcars of the train. Good cowpokes could load 30 to 40 head of cattle into one boxcar by poking them into the correct position.

Some of the ranchers would tip, or cut off the sharp points of the cattle horns so that they reduced the possibility of cutting up the hides of other cattle, damaging their meat, or the physical objects such as the boxcar, or working pens. This was done with a horn tipper that resembles and works like a very large nail clipper, and just cuts the tip end off. This doesn't hurt the cattle as their horns are like huge toenails and there are no nerves in the tips of the horn. Other ranchers would cut the horns off of the cattle using hand saws which causes a lot of bleeding and opens the site for infection. They would then apply a hot cauterizing iron followed with a big smear of pine tar. This was a rare practice as the horns had value as well, not only for decorative wall displays, but furniture, drinking gourds, and other household items made out of the horns.

**Photo**: Cowpokes assisting the organized loading of the big Texas Longhorn cattle onto the boxcar of a train for shipping. Courtesy of John Bintliff.

Even without these techniques being applied to the horns, the Texas Longhorn is pretty careful when moving through heavy brush country, walking through gates and fenced areas, and even entering and exiting boxcars, working chutes, or the more modern squeeze chutes.

The cowboy uses these pens for sorting and separating cattle for various reasons and doctoring as well.

**Photo**: Jim Hodges and his horse, Buck, sort out a young Longhorn for doctoring. Photo courtesy of Gleaves Whitney.

One of the young cowboys who worked for me, Tom Nesser, was eager to demonstrate his skills and value during a cattle roundup and working one hot summer day. We had penned what cattle we could find in the open and were headed back to the brushy areas for strays. Using my binoculars, I spotted a group of Texas Longhorn females hiding in the high vegetation and trees along a muddy creek roughly 200 yards ahead of us. Hearing the news, young Tom quickly stated, " I'll get 'em outa there boss, my horse is plenty fast enough to catch 'em when they break into the open". Well, he was there to work, but also to learn, so I allowed him the privilege of demonstrating his skill stating, " Okay Tom, ride 'em out, son. Jack, Spud, and Harb will pick up your flanks in the open and slow 'em down towards the pens". I had no sooner completed the orders when Tom spurred his horse on at a slow lope and disappeared into the bean trees on their oblique. An eerie quiet set over the plain – suddenly broken by what sounded like a cross between a Comanche on the charge, and a baby dropped on its head! The outlying high brush exploded as if spitting Tom and his horse back into the pasture with the loud swish of crumpling plants and loud cracking noise of saplings snapping. From that great distance I could make out Tom's eyes bulged wide and his mouth flapping forming the unidentifiable screams we had heard. Tom's horse was in a flat-out dead run toward the open fields with Tom's legs spurring for all he was worth. As Tom passed us by I yelled at the other cowboys, " Let him go, we got work to do"! With the more experienced cowboys finishing the job and the day drawing to an end we all met around the chucktruck which was parked by the line camp. As the campfire glowed and some beans and cornbread were being devoured Tom remained quiet and resigned. It was the cook, Ole Raul, who finally spoke up, " Well Tom, I heard-tell that old horse of yours could outrun Seabiscuit". Everyone laughed except Tom, who was obviously embarrassed but the cowboys were certainly understanding. I looked at Tom and stated, " I suppose those old Longhorns taught you that they don't all run away from you…some of 'em run right at you". Tom appreciated the counseling and camaraderie and showed great character by affirming, " I've sure learned a lesson today that I won't forget the next time. I never want to face those huge chargin' horns again"! Of course, we've all faced them once, and again. It is the nature of the Texas Longhorn.

**Photo:** Jim Hodges and his horse, Carlos, pen young Longhorns. Photo courtesy, Nellie Connally, Former First Lady of Texas, from her book, *Houston City in Motion*. Her husband was former Texas Governor John Connally.

**Photo**: Texas Longhorn youngsters. By Jim Hodges.


When the Texas Longhorn cattle are handled from birth, as these youngsters were, they become docile and accommodating, as seen pulling the wagons for settlers across the West and also became valued pets to some.

# Texas Longhorns as Pets, Mascots, Friends

**Photo:** Longhorn Oxen Pulling Wagon. Kansas Historical Records.

**Photo**: "Bevo", Mascot of the University of Texas Longhorns. Courtesy, www.utexas.edu.

**Photo:** Tex McDaniel rode from Houston to New York City, and then on to Washington D.C. on his Texas Longhorn steer named, Barker in 1932 - 1933.

**Photo**: The Fort Worth Herd driving Texas Longhorns down N. Exchange Avenue. Courtesy, Jim Hodges.

The Fort Worth Herd brings Texas cattle drive history to life twice a day on the very street leading to the Fort Worth Stockyards which was the trailhead for many cattle drives from the post-Civil War era. Here, visitors from every corner of the globe can get an up-close look at the Texas Longhorns and the drovers that brought them to the stockyards in the period of the Old West. Drover was another term for a cowboy who rode horseback moving cattle up the long trails, and the Fort Worth Herd represents that historical accuracy in every detail.

- Reference: www.fortworth.com/the-herd

J. Frank Dobie wrote in his book, "However supplanted or however disparaged by evolving standards and generations, he will remain the bedrock on which the history of the cow country of America is founded. In picturesqueness and romantic realism, his name is destined for remembrance as long as the memory of man travels back to those pristine times when waters ran clear, when free grass waved a carpet over the face of the earth, and America's Man on Horseback--not a helmeted soldier, but a booted cowboy-- rode over the rim with all the abandon, energy, insolence, pride, carelessness and confidence epitomizing the booming West". **Reference:** *J. Frank Dobie, The Longhorns. Austin, Texas: University of Texas Press.*

Such stories are so plentiful and beautifully written by so many authors, poets, songwriters, and plain-put storytellers. They are heartfelt, and almost reverend even in the literal or scholarly form. No other cattle breed has taught so much history to so many around the world as the Texas Longhorn, and no other breed has been pointed out as the suspect of teaching the world about the cowboy. They now share their unique legends, one complementing the other.

No other breed of cattle has ever been so well known or instantly recognizable across their home range, and even the entire globe as the Texas Longhorn. To encounter them in the wild is to instantly visualize their history and the rawest of the natural elements.

**Photo:** Texas cowboys holding Longhorn cattle. DeGolyer Library, Southern Methodist University, 1900 photo.

# The Science

Ironically, the modern age of the genome has confirmed the global link to the history of the Longhorn, and in that revelation may exist a credible piece of evidence for my thesis of the spirit walkers. Perhaps the senses can hear the 30,000-year-old spirits of their ancestors as their own. This could explain why humans and even other animals, act differently around them. They seem to relate without a proper introduction.

The published results in 2013 from David Hillis, a University of Texas biologist and geneticist who was spearheading the year-long study of the Longhorn genome studied some 48,000 genetic markers of DNA from 58 cattle breeds. The results confirm that the Longhorns of the western world are direct descendants of Spanish cattle brought by Christopher Columbus to Hispaniola in 1493. Spanish colonists traveled to Mexico in 1521 bringing the descendants of those cattle with them. Some were left, or escaped into the wild and eventually migrated to present-day Texas.

The study's DNA evidence traces Longhorn cattle ancestry back as far as 30,000 years to cattle in the Middle East, India, and Pakistan. Africa became the convergence of these breeds where they eventually adapted to hot, and dry climate, and developed resistance to disease.

According to Hillis, their new research reveals that 15 percent of the genetic makeup of Longhorns reflects the India-Africa influence. This creates the possibility that Moors brought African cattle with them during their invasion of Spain from the eighth to the 13th centuries. Another possibility is that these cattle were imported from Africa to the Canary Islands, where Columbus probably loaded them on his ships and headed for the New World. It was estimated that by 1690, the Longhorn had made its' nascence into what is now known as Texas.

As the long cattle drives almost eliminated Longhorns by the turn of the 20th century, the U.S. government, in 1927 joined by Texas, began working to preserve the Longhorn cattle. Finally, in the 1960s, the Texas Longhorn Breeders Association of America was founded and began to register the Longhorn breed. At the formation of the registry, it was estimated that only 1,500 head of true Longhorn cattle were still extant. Today, it is hard to estimate how many Longhorn cattle exist, but they are truly valuable and profitable continuing to yield lean good tasting beef.

- **Reference**: news.edu.utexas,edu, May 26, 2013. David Hillis Team.

What history has presumed and modern teams of researchers have confirmed was most certainly known even to the mettlesome villagers and pioneers who first laid eyes on Longhorn cattle by the shear visage of their form against the inured terrain they adapted to so well. Through the desperate partnership, they grew together and drifted across the plains, adding value to every culture.

# Interesting Details

Texas Longhorn cattle eat grass as most cattle do, but they are unique in the way they created themselves into ingenious foragers when grass wasn't so plentiful, and water was in short supply. They have a keen set of senses that can smell water a mile or more away, and locate small plants and various scraps of cactus and weeds to keep themselves going when other cattle would certainly perish. In fact, the Texas Longhorn cattle survived the worst drought in Texas history by eating cactus.

They really flourish on good grass and do not need a man-made feed of any kind to stay fat enough for the females to calve, feeder steers to bring good prices at the sales, and very tasty beef for the table. Its high levels of protein despite the dramatic decrease in saturated animal fats, soluble fatty acids, and cholesterol make it comparable to skinless baked chicken. Ranchers in the current market will supplement them with hay in the form of round or square bales, range cubes, which is a compressed pellet, silage, which is a type of fodder made of green foliage crops which have been preserved by acidification achieved through fermentation, or, in some cases a grain mixed food source. As they are also more resistant to disease than other breeds, they are referred to as, *easy keepers*. Many of the old-time ranchers would attest, " Just put 'em out there and forget 'em. Next Spring, you'll have some new calves on the ground."

Their longevity is unequal in the cattle world as generally a lifespan of 20 – 30 years is commonplace. Many ranchers and cowboys can attest to Longhorns living into their 30s. Another benefit to the rancher is that the females can produce as many as 20 calves in their lifetime, and have very few problems with pregnancy or birth. Their pregnancy is between 285 to 295 days, and they produce calves of good birth weights and the mothers are good milkers as well. Other breeds of cattle might have cows produce 10 to 14 babies in their lifetime, so the benefit is obvious.

The U.S. Meat Animal Research Center at Clay Center, Nebraska has tested the Texas Longhorn breed's modern qualities, "Their Germ Plasm Evaluation Program, Cycle IV Phase 2, evaluated 1,905 births comparing 11 breeds. The Texas Longhorn proved superior with the highest unassisted birth rate of all breeds (99.7%) and the lowest birth weight (71.3 lbs.)." The offspring is hearty and able to actually stand and nurse their mother within 10 minutes of birth. They will lay close to their mother and build strength over a few weeks before beginning their exploration of their pastures and surroundings. It has been recorded that a Longhorn female calf can conceive as early as 18 months, so maturity is also on the list of their strong characteristics!

Wild and varied colors of their hide are unique to the breed as there are no two alike, and even twins have individual colors and patterns. The speculation through evidence is that their genetics from ancient times show through with each baby born wrapped in its unique color. The adult Longhorn can grow to be as tall as 4 to 6 feet at the shoulder, have a horn spread of 8 to 10 feet, and weigh in at 800 to 1500 pounds.

The horns are fascinating and certainly one of the more prevalent mysteries. A careful study of them reveals that they are either indicative of their bloodlines, reshaped by an accident, or shaped by the rancher by use of horn weights. Each family of Longhorns has a peculiar size, shape, twist, and color. As you have seen in the photos provided, most of the horn sets are genetic and symmetrical, however, there are anomalies. Damage that is not too severe can cause one horn, or the other to grow back crooked, pointing in the opposite direction than the other horn. Ranchers sometimes would use horn weights to make unique horn curls, or droops for decorative purposes. Horn weights are screwed onto the horns at an early age, and as they grow, the horns begin to slowly curl, or curve.

African cattle such as the Watusi and Ankole are sometimes put on display, or mistaken for Longhorn cattle. They are recognizable quickly as their horns look too disproportionate to their bodies, or have wild droops, or face straight up into the air. To study the Longhorn horns in-depth you can navigate to this website for a great reference and well-written history of the Longhorn.

- **Reference**: http://longhornmuseum.com/index.htm

**Photo:** Longhorns at Sunset, by Jim Hodges. Taken on the George Ranch Richmond, Texas.

# Sequitur

If I have proven my case to hold some ounce of validity in your mind through this research, and your soul through the spiritual thesis, then I have been successful in my ultimate goal of entertaining as well as enlightening you.  In the amazement of the modern-day pilgrim at the first glimpse of a Texas Longhorn lies the self-evident proof that they are truly spirit walkers and storytellers of olden times. If you skillfully listen to their silent conversations about the experience and the details that they notice, you can hear the lessons and mystic contact taking hold of them. There, they remain for the rest of their lives, and within the repeated stories of those who have spent their lives among them.

Perhaps if the mighty Texas Longhorn could speak they would offer a short dose of prose:

" I am history. In my eye, I keep the stories of long times gone. Only the Chiefs can hear the stories, in the silence of the night – where the wind preaches them. They have gone out and told them to the tribes of man who will listen. Before those who can speak words, I was here – roaming the eroded escarpments, and grazing the rich arroyo. I am history…. listen to the wind…"

**Photo**: Texas Longhorn grazing by Jim Hodges, 2008. Stonewall, Texas.

# Interesting References and links

- James Westfall Thompson, History of Livestock Raising in the United States, 1607-1860 (Washington: U.S. Department of Agriculture, 1942).

- James Frank Dobie, The Longhorns (Austin, Texas: University of Texas Press, 1980) (ISBN 029274627X).

- Don Worcester, The Texas Longhorn: Relic of the Past, Asset for the Future (College Station: Texas A&M University Press, 1987) (ISBN 0890966257)

- The University of Texas at Austin (March 25, 2013). "Decoding the genetic history of the Texas longhorn". ScienceDaily. Retrieved April 7, 2013.

- "Longhorn Cattle," Handbook of Texas Online. Published by the Texas State Historical Association.

- https://www.thc.texas.gov/historic-sites/fort-griffin/history/legendary-longhorns, The Official Texas State Longhorn Herd at Fort Griffin.

- https://tpwd.texas.gov/state-parks/park-information/official-state-longhorn, Texas Longhorns in State Parks.